Reading Journal

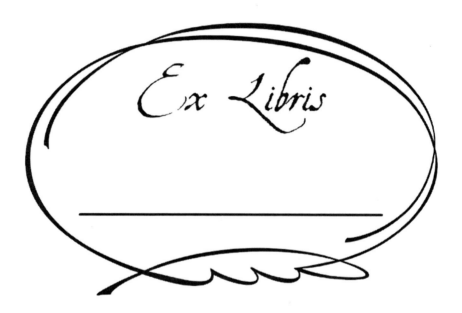

Ex Libris

Cover Art and Interior Design: Cheryl Casey
copyright © 2014 by Cheryl Casey

Wingfeather Books
™

wingfeatherbooks.com

Title: _____

Author: _____

Date finished: _____

Note or Favorite passage: _____

_____

_____

_____

Title: _____

Author: _____

Date finished: _____

Note or Favorite passage: _____

_____

_____

_____

Title: _____

Author: _____

Date finished: _____

Note or Favorite passage: _____

_____

_____

_____

Title: _____

Author: _____

Date finished: _____

Note or Favorite passage: _____

_____

_____

_____

Title: _____

Author: _____

Date finished: _____

Note or Favorite passage: _____

_____

_____

_____

Title: _____

Author: _____

Date finished: _____

Note or Favorite passage: _____

_____

_____

_____

Title: _____

Author: _____

Date finished: _____

Note or Favorite passage: _____

_____

_____

_____

Title: _____

Author: _____

Date finished: _____

Note or Favorite passage: _____

_____

_____

_____

Title: _____

Author: _____

Date finished: _____

Note or Favorite passage: _____

_____

_____

_____

Title: _____

Author: _____

Date finished: _____

Note or Favorite passage: _____

_____

_____

_____

Title: _____

Author: _____

Date finished: _____

Note or Favorite passage: _____

_____

_____

_____

Title: _____

Author: _____

Date finished: _____

Note or Favorite passage: _____

_____

_____

_____

Title: _____

Author: _____

Date finished: _____

Note or Favorite passage: _____

_____

_____

_____

Title: _____

Author: _____

Date finished: _____

Note or Favorite passage: _____

_____

_____

_____

Title: _____

Author: _____

Date finished: _____

Note or Favorite passage: _____

_____

_____

_____

Title: _____

Author: _____

Date finished: _____

Note or Favorite passage: _____

_____

_____

_____

Title: _____

Author: _____

Date finished: _____

Note or Favorite passage: _____

_____

_____

_____

Title: _____

Author: _____

Date finished: _____

Note or Favorite passage: _____

_____

_____

_____

Title: _____

Author: _____

Date finished: _____

Note or Favorite passage: _____

_____

_____

_____

Title: _____

Author: _____

Date finished: _____

Note or Favorite passage: _____

_____

_____

_____

Title: _____

Author: _____

Date finished: _____

Note or Favorite passage: _____

_____

_____

_____

Title: _____

Author: _____

Date finished: _____

Note or Favorite passage: _____

_____

_____

_____

Title: _____

Author: _____

Date finished: _____

Note or Favorite passage: _____

_____

_____

_____

Title: _____

Author: _____

Date finished: _____

Note or Favorite passage: _____

_____

_____

_____

Title: _____

Author: _____

Date finished: _____

Note or Favorite passage: _____

_____

_____

_____

Title: _____

Author: _____

Date finished: _____

Note or Favorite passage: _____

_____

_____

_____

Title: _____

Author: _____

Date finished: _____

Note or Favorite passage: _____

_____

_____

_____

Title: _____

Author: _____

Date finished: _____

Note or Favorite passage: _____

_____

_____

_____

Title: _____

Author: _____

Date finished: _____

Note or Favorite passage: _____

_____

_____

_____

Title: _____

Author: _____

Date finished: _____

Note or Favorite passage: _____

_____

_____

_____

Title: _____

Author: _____

Date finished: _____

Note or Favorite passage: _____

_____

_____

_____

Title: _____

Author: _____

Date finished: _____

Note or Favorite passage: _____

_____

_____

_____

Title: _____

Author: _____

Date finished: _____

Note or Favorite passage: _____

_____

_____

_____

Title: _____

Author: _____

Date finished: _____

Note or Favorite passage: _____

_____

_____

_____

Title: _____

Author: _____

Date finished: _____

Note or Favorite passage: _____

_____

_____

_____

Title: _____

Author: _____

Date finished: _____

Note or Favorite passage: _____

_____

_____

_____

Title: _____

Author: _____

Date finished: _____

Note or Favorite passage: _____

_____

_____

_____

Title: _____

Author: _____

Date finished: _____

Note or Favorite passage: _____

_____

_____

_____

Title: _____

Author: _____

Date finished: _____

Note or Favorite passage: _____

_____

_____

_____

Title: _____

Author: _____

Date finished: _____

Note or Favorite passage: _____

_____

_____

_____

Title: _____

Author: _____

Date finished: _____

Note or Favorite passage: _____

_____

_____

_____

Title: _____

Author: _____

Date finished: _____

Note or Favorite passage: _____

_____

_____

_____

Title: _____

Author: _____

Date finished: _____

Note or Favorite passage: _____

_____

_____

_____

Title: _____

Author: _____

Date finished: _____

Note or Favorite passage: _____

_____

_____

_____

Title: _____

Author: _____

Date finished: _____

Note or Favorite passage: _____

_____

_____

_____

Title: _____

Author: _____

Date finished: _____

Note or Favorite passage: _____

_____

_____

_____

Title: _____

Author: _____

Date finished: _____

Note or Favorite passage: _____

_____

_____

_____

Title: _____

Author: _____

Date finished: _____

Note or Favorite passage: _____

_____

_____

_____

Title: _____

Author: _____

Date finished: _____

Note or Favorite passage: _____

_____

_____

_____

Title: _____

Author: _____

Date finished: _____

Note or Favorite passage: _____

_____

_____

_____

Title: _____

Author: _____

Date finished: _____

Note or Favorite passage: _____

_____

_____

_____

Title: _____

Author: _____

Date finished: _____

Note or Favorite passage: _____

_____

_____

_____

Title: _____

Author: _____

Date finished: _____

Note or Favorite passage: _____

_____

_____

_____

Title: _____

Author: _____

Date finished: _____

Note or Favorite passage: _____

_____

_____

_____

Title: _____

Author: _____

Date finished: _____

Note or Favorite passage: _____

_____

_____

_____

Title: _____

Author: _____

Date finished: _____

Note or Favorite passage: _____

_____

_____

_____

Title: _____

Author: _____

Date finished: _____

Note or Favorite passage: _____

_____

_____

_____

Title: _____

Author: _____

Date finished: _____

Note or Favorite passage: _____

_____

_____

_____

Title: _____

Author: _____

Date finished: _____

Note or Favorite passage: _____

_____

_____

_____

Title: _____

Author: _____

Date finished: _____

Note or Favorite passage: _____

_____

_____

_____

Title: _____

Author: _____

Date finished: _____

Note or Favorite passage: _____

_____

_____

_____

Title: _____

Author: _____

Date finished: _____

Note or Favorite passage: _____

_____

_____

_____

Title: _____

Author: _____

Date finished: _____

Note or Favorite passage: _____

_____

_____

_____

Title: _____

Author: _____

Date finished: _____

Note or Favorite passage: _____

_____

_____

_____

Title: _____

Author: _____

Date finished: _____

Note or Favorite passage: _____

_____

_____

_____

Title: _____

Author: _____

Date finished: _____

Note or Favorite passage: _____

_____

_____

_____

Title: _____

Author: _____

Date finished: _____

Note or Favorite passage: _____

_____

_____

_____

Title: _____

Author: _____

Date finished: _____

Note or Favorite passage: _____

_____

_____

_____

Title: _____

Author: _____

Date finished: _____

Note or Favorite passage: _____

_____

_____

_____

Title: _____

Author: _____

Date finished: _____

Note or Favorite passage: _____

_____

_____

_____

Title: _____

Author: _____

Date finished: _____

Note or Favorite passage: _____

_____

_____

_____

Title: _____

Author: _____

Date finished: _____

Note or Favorite passage: _____

_____

_____

_____

Title: _____

Author: _____

Date finished: _____

Note or Favorite passage: _____

_____

_____

_____

Title: _____

Author: _____

Date finished: _____

Note or Favorite passage: _____

_____

_____

_____

Title: _____

Author: _____

Date finished: _____

Note or Favorite passage: _____

_____

_____

_____

Title: _____

Author: _____

Date finished: _____

Note or Favorite passage: _____

_____

_____

_____

Title: _____

Author: _____

Date finished: _____

Note or Favorite passage: _____

_____

_____

_____

Title: _____

Author: _____

Date finished: _____

Note or Favorite passage: _____

_____

_____

_____

Title: _____

Author: _____

Date finished: _____

Note or Favorite passage: _____

_____

_____

_____

Title: _____

Author: _____

Date finished: _____

Note or Favorite passage: _____

_____

_____

_____

Title: _____

Author: _____

Date finished: _____

Note or Favorite passage: _____

_____

_____

_____

Title: _____

Author: _____

Date finished: _____

Note or Favorite passage: _____

_____

_____

_____

Title: _____

Author: _____

Date finished: _____

Note or Favorite passage: _____

_____

_____

_____

Title: _____

Author: _____

Date finished: _____

Note or Favorite passage: _____

_____

_____

_____

Title: _____

Author: _____

Date finished: _____

Note or Favorite passage: _____

_____

_____

_____

Title: _____

Author: _____

Date finished: _____

Note or Favorite passage: _____

_____

_____

_____

Title: _____

Author: _____

Date finished: _____

Note or Favorite passage: _____

_____

_____

_____

Title: _____

Author: _____

Date finished: _____

Note or Favorite passage: _____

_____

_____

_____

Title: _____

Author: _____

Date finished: _____

Note or Favorite passage: _____

_____

_____

_____

Title: _____

Author: _____

Date finished: _____

Note or Favorite passage: _____

_____

_____

_____

Title: _____

Author: _____

Date finished: _____

Note or Favorite passage: _____

_____

_____

_____

Title: _____

Author: _____

Date finished: _____

Note or Favorite passage: _____

_____

_____

_____

Title: _____

Author: _____

Date finished: _____

Note or Favorite passage: _____

_____

_____

_____

Title: _____

Author: _____

Date finished: _____

Note or Favorite passage: _____

_____

_____

_____

Title: _____

Author: _____

Date finished: _____

Note or Favorite passage: _____

_____

_____

_____

Title: _____

Author: _____

Date finished: _____

Note or Favorite passage: _____

_____

_____

_____

Title: _____

Author: _____

Date finished: _____

Note or Favorite passage: _____

_____

_____

_____

Title: _____

Author: _____

Date finished: _____

Note or Favorite passage: _____

_____

_____

_____

Title: _____

Author: _____

Date finished: _____

Note or Favorite passage: _____

_____

_____

_____

Title: _____

Author: _____

Date finished: _____

Note or Favorite passage: _____

_____

_____

_____

Title: _____

Author: _____

Date finished: _____

Note or Favorite passage: _____

_____

_____

_____

Title: _____

Author: _____

Date finished: _____

Note or Favorite passage: _____

_____

_____

_____

Title: _____

Author: _____

Date finished: _____

Note or Favorite passage: _____

_____

_____

_____

Title: _____

Author: _____

Date finished: _____

Note or Favorite passage: _____

_____

_____

_____

Title: _____

Author: _____

Date finished: _____

Note or Favorite passage: _____

_____

_____

_____

Title: _____

Author: _____

Date finished: _____

Note or Favorite passage: _____

_____

_____

_____

Title: _____

Author: _____

Date finished: _____

Note or Favorite passage: _____

_____

_____

_____

Title: _____

Author: _____

Date finished: _____

Note or Favorite passage: _____

_____

_____

_____

Title: _____

Author: _____

Date finished: _____

Note or Favorite passage: _____

_____

_____

_____

Title: _____

Author: _____

Date finished: _____

Note or Favorite passage: _____

_____

_____

_____

Title: _____

Author: _____

Date finished: _____

Note or Favorite passage: _____

_____

_____

_____

Title: _____

Author: _____

Date finished: _____

Note or Favorite passage: _____

_____

_____

_____

Title: _____

Author: _____

Date finished: _____

Note or Favorite passage: _____

_____

_____

_____

Title: _____

Author: _____

Date finished: _____

Note or Favorite passage: _____

_____

_____

_____

Title: _____

Author: _____

Date finished: _____

Note or Favorite passage: _____

_____

_____

_____

Title: _____

Author: _____

Date finished: _____

Note or Favorite passage: _____

_____

_____

_____

Title: _____

Author: _____

Date finished: _____

Note or Favorite passage: _____

_____

_____

_____

Title: _____

Author: _____

Date finished: _____

Note or Favorite passage: _____

_____

_____

_____

Title: _____

Author: _____

Date finished: _____

Note or Favorite passage: _____

_____

_____

_____

Title: _____

Author: _____

Date finished: _____

Note or Favorite passage: _____

_____

_____

_____

Title: _____

Author: _____

Date finished: _____

Note or Favorite passage: _____

_____

_____

_____

Title: _____

Author: _____

Date finished: _____

Note or Favorite passage: _____

_____

_____

_____

Title: _____

Author: _____

Date finished: _____

Note or Favorite passage: _____

_____

_____

_____

Title: _____

Author: _____

Date finished: _____

Note or Favorite passage: _____

_____

_____

_____

Title: _____

Author: _____

Date finished: _____

Note or Favorite passage: _____

_____

_____

_____

Title: _____

Author: _____

Date finished: _____

Note or Favorite passage: _____

_____

_____

_____

Title: _____

Author: _____

Date finished: _____

Note or Favorite passage: _____

_____

_____

_____

Title: _____

Author: _____

Date finished: _____

Note or Favorite passage: _____

_____

_____

_____

Title: _____

Author: _____

Date finished: _____

Note or Favorite passage: _____

_____

_____

_____

Title: _____

Author: _____

Date finished: _____

Note or Favorite passage: _____

_____

_____

_____

Title: _____

Author: _____

Date finished: _____

Note or Favorite passage: _____

_____

_____

_____

Title: _____

Author: _____

Date finished: _____

Note or Favorite passage: _____

_____

_____

_____

Title: _____

Author: _____

Date finished: _____

Note or Favorite passage: _____

_____

_____

_____

Title: _____

Author: _____

Date finished: _____

Note or Favorite passage: _____

_____

_____

_____

Title: _____

Author: _____

Date finished: _____

Note or Favorite passage: _____

_____

_____

_____

Title: _____

Author: _____

Date finished: _____

Note or Favorite passage: _____

_____

_____

_____

Title: _____

Author: _____

Date finished: _____

Note or Favorite passage: _____

_____

_____

_____

Title: _____

Author: _____

Date finished: _____

Note or Favorite passage: _____

_____

_____

_____

Title: _____

Author: _____

Date finished: _____

Note or Favorite passage: _____

_____

_____

_____

Title: _____

Author: _____

Date finished: _____

Note or Favorite passage: _____

_____

_____

_____

Title: _____

Author: _____

Date finished: _____

Note or Favorite passage: _____

_____

_____

_____

Title: _____

Author: _____

Date finished: _____

Note or Favorite passage: _____

_____

_____

_____

Title: _____

Author: _____

Date finished: _____

Note or Favorite passage: _____

_____

_____

_____

Title: _____

Author: _____

Date finished: _____

Note or Favorite passage: _____

_____

_____

_____

Title: _____

Author: _____

Date finished: _____

Note or Favorite passage: _____

_____

_____

_____

Title: _____

Author: _____

Date finished: _____

Note or Favorite passage: _____

_____

_____

_____

Title: _____

Author: _____

Date finished: _____

Note or Favorite passage: _____

_____

_____

_____

Title: _____

Author: _____

Date finished: _____

Note or Favorite passage: _____

_____

_____

_____

Title: _____

Author: _____

Date finished: _____

Note or Favorite passage: _____

_____

_____

_____

Title: _____

Author: _____

Date finished: _____

Note or Favorite passage: _____

_____

_____

_____

Title: _____

Author: _____

Date finished: _____

Note or Favorite passage: _____

_____

_____

_____

Title: _____

Author: _____

Date finished: _____

Note or Favorite passage: _____

_____

_____

_____

Title: _____

Author: _____

Date finished: _____

Note or Favorite passage: _____

_____

_____

_____

Title: _____

Author: _____

Date finished: _____

Note or Favorite passage: _____

_____

_____

_____

Title: _____

Author: _____

Date finished: _____

Note or Favorite passage: _____

_____

_____

_____

Title: _____

Author: _____

Date finished: _____

Note or Favorite passage: _____

_____

_____

_____

Title: _____

Author: _____

Date finished: _____

Note or Favorite passage: _____

_____

_____

_____

Title: _____

Author: _____

Date finished: _____

Note or Favorite passage: _____

_____

_____

_____

Title: _____

Author: _____

Date finished: _____

Note or Favorite passage: _____

_____

_____

_____

Title: _____

Author: _____

Date finished: _____

Note or Favorite passage: _____

_____

_____

_____

Title: _____

Author: _____

Date finished: _____

Note or Favorite passage: _____

_____

_____

_____

Title: _____

Author: _____

Date finished: _____

Note or Favorite passage: _____

_____

_____

_____

Title: _____

Author: _____

Date finished: _____

Note or Favorite passage: _____

_____

_____

_____

Title: _____

Author: _____

Date finished: _____

Note or Favorite passage: _____

_____

_____

_____

Title: _____

Author: _____

Date finished: _____

Note or Favorite passage: _____

_____

_____

_____

Title: _____

Author: _____

Date finished: _____

Note or Favorite passage: _____

_____

_____

_____

Title: _____

Author: _____

Date finished: _____

Note or Favorite passage: _____

_____

_____

_____

Title: _____

Author: _____

Date finished: _____

Note or Favorite passage: _____

_____

_____

_____

Title: _____

Author: _____

Date finished: _____

Note or Favorite passage: _____

_____

_____

_____

Title: _____

Author: _____

Date finished: _____

Note or Favorite passage: _____

_____

_____

_____

Title: _____

Author: _____

Date finished: _____

Note or Favorite passage: _____

_____

_____

_____

Title: _____

Author: _____

Date finished: _____

Note or Favorite passage: _____

_____

_____

_____

Title: _____

Author: _____

Date finished: _____

Note or Favorite passage: _____

_____

_____

_____

Title: _____

Author: _____

Date finished: _____

Note or Favorite passage: _____

_____

_____

_____

Title: _____

Author: _____

Date finished: _____

Note or Favorite passage: _____

_____

_____

_____

Title: _____

Author: _____

Date finished: _____

Note or Favorite passage: _____

_____

_____

_____

Title: _____

Author: _____

Date finished: _____

Note or Favorite passage: _____

_____

_____

_____

Title: _____

Author: _____

Date finished: _____

Note or Favorite passage: _____

_____

_____

_____

Title: _____

Author: _____

Date finished: _____

Note or Favorite passage: _____

_____

_____

_____

Title: _____

Author: _____

Date finished: _____

Note or Favorite passage: _____

_____

_____

_____

Title: _____

Author: _____

Date finished: _____

Note or Favorite passage: _____

_____

_____

_____

Title: _____

Author: _____

Date finished: _____

Note or Favorite passage: _____

_____

_____

_____

Title: _____

Author: _____

Date finished: _____

Note or Favorite passage: _____

_____

_____

_____

Title: _____

Author: _____

Date finished: _____

Note or Favorite passage: _____

_____

_____

_____

Title: _____

Author: _____

Date finished: _____

Note or Favorite passage: _____

_____

_____

_____

Title: _____

Author: _____

Date finished: _____

Note or Favorite passage: _____

_____

_____

_____

Title: _____

Author: _____

Date finished: _____

Note or Favorite passage: _____

_____

_____

_____

Title: _____

Author: _____

Date finished: _____

Note or Favorite passage: _____

_____

_____

_____

Title: _____

Author: _____

Date finished: _____

Note or Favorite passage: _____

_____

_____

_____

Title: _____

Author: _____

Date finished: _____

Note or Favorite passage: _____

_____

_____

_____

Title: _____

Author: _____

Date finished: _____

Note or Favorite passage: _____

_____

_____

_____

Title: _____

Author: _____

Date finished: _____

Note or Favorite passage: _____

_____

_____

_____

Title: _____

Author: _____

Date finished: _____

Note or Favorite passage: _____

_____

_____

_____

Title: _____

Author: _____

Date finished: _____

Note or Favorite passage: _____

_____

_____

_____

Title: _____

Author: _____

Date finished: _____

Note or Favorite passage: _____

_____

_____

_____

Title: _____

Author: _____

Date finished: _____

Note or Favorite passage: _____

_____

_____

_____

Title: _____

Author: _____

Date finished: _____

Note or Favorite passage: _____

_____

_____

_____

Title: _____

Author: _____

Date finished: _____

Note or Favorite passage: _____

_____

_____

_____

Title: _____

Author: _____

Date finished: _____

Note or Favorite passage: _____

_____

_____

_____

Title: _____

Author: _____

Date finished: _____

Note or Favorite passage: _____

_____

_____

_____

Title: _____

Author: _____

Date finished: _____

Note or Favorite passage: _____

_____

_____

_____

Title: _____

Author: _____

Date finished: _____

Note or Favorite passage: _____

_____

_____

_____

Title: _____

Author: _____

Date finished: _____

Note or Favorite passage: _____

_____

_____

_____

Title: _____

Author: _____

Date finished: _____

Note or Favorite passage: _____

_____

_____

_____

Title: _____

Author: _____

Date finished: _____

Note or Favorite passage: _____

_____

_____

_____

Title: _____

Author: _____

Date finished: _____

Note or Favorite passage: _____

_____

_____

_____

Title: _____

Author: _____

Date finished: _____

Note or Favorite passage: _____

_____

_____

_____

Title: _____

Author: _____

Date finished: _____

Note or Favorite passage: _____

_____

_____

_____

Title: _____

Author: _____

Date finished: _____

Note or Favorite passage: _____

_____

_____

_____

Title: _____

Author: _____

Date finished: _____

Note or Favorite passage: _____

_____

_____

_____

Title: _____

Author: _____

Date finished: _____

Note or Favorite passage: _____

_____

_____

_____

Title: _____

Author: _____

Date finished: _____

Note or Favorite passage: _____

_____

_____

_____

Title: _____

Author: _____

Date finished: _____

Note or Favorite passage: _____

_____

_____

_____

Title: _____

Author: _____

Date finished: _____

Note or Favorite passage: _____

_____

_____

_____

Title: _____

Author: _____

Date finished: _____

Note or Favorite passage: _____

_____

_____

_____

Title: _____

Author: _____

Date finished: _____

Note or Favorite passage: _____

_____

_____

_____

Title: _____

Author: _____

Date finished: _____

Note or Favorite passage: _____

_____

_____

_____

Title: _____

Author: _____

Date finished: _____

Note or Favorite passage: _____

_____

_____

_____

Title: _____

Author: _____

Date finished: _____

Note or Favorite passage: _____

_____

_____

_____

Title: _____

Author: _____

Date finished: _____

Note or Favorite passage: _____

_____

_____

_____

Title: _____

Author: _____

Date finished: _____

Note or Favorite passage: _____

_____

_____

_____

Title: _____

Author: _____

Date finished: _____

Note or Favorite passage: _____

_____

_____

_____

Title: _____

Author: _____

Date finished: _____

Note or Favorite passage: _____

_____

_____

_____

Title: _____

Author: _____

Date finished: _____

Note or Favorite passage: _____

_____

_____

_____

Title: _____

Author: _____

Date finished: _____

Note or Favorite passage: _____

_____

_____

_____

Title: _____

Author: _____

Date finished: _____

Note or Favorite passage: _____

_____

_____

_____

Title: _____

Author: _____

Date finished: _____

Note or Favorite passage: _____

_____

_____

_____

Title: _____

Author: _____

Date finished: _____

Note or Favorite passage: _____

_____

_____

_____

Title: _____

Author: _____

Date finished: _____

Note or Favorite passage: _____

_____

_____

_____

Title: _____

Author: _____

Date finished: _____

Note or Favorite passage: _____

_____

_____

_____

Title: _____

Author: _____

Date finished: _____

Note or Favorite passage: _____

_____

_____

_____

Title: _____

Author: _____

Date finished: _____

Note or Favorite passage: _____

_____

_____

_____

Title: _____

Author: _____

Date finished: _____

Note or Favorite passage: _____

_____

_____

_____

Title: _____

Author: _____

Date finished: _____

Note or Favorite passage: _____

_____

_____

_____

Title: _____

Author: _____

Date finished: _____

Note or Favorite passage: _____

_____

_____

_____

Title: _____

Author: _____

Date finished: _____

Note or Favorite passage: _____

_____

_____

_____

Title: _____

Author: _____

Date finished: _____

Note or Favorite passage: _____

_____

_____

_____

Title: _____

Author: _____

Date finished: _____

Note or Favorite passage: _____

_____

_____

_____

Title: _____

Author: _____

Date finished: _____

Note or Favorite passage: _____

_____

_____

_____

Title: _____

Author: _____

Date finished: _____

Note or Favorite passage: _____

_____

_____

_____

Title: _____

Author: _____

Date finished: _____

Note or Favorite passage: _____

_____

_____

_____

Title: _____

Author: _____

Date finished: _____

Note or Favorite passage: _____

_____

_____

_____

Title: _____

Author: _____

Date finished: _____

Note or Favorite passage: _____

_____

_____

_____

Title: _____

Author: _____

Date finished: _____

Note or Favorite passage: _____

_____

_____

_____

Title: _____

Author: _____

Date finished: _____

Note or Favorite passage: _____

_____

_____

_____

Title: _____

Author: _____

Date finished: _____

Note or Favorite passage: _____

_____

_____

_____

Title: _____

Author: _____

Date finished: _____

Note or Favorite passage: _____

_____

_____

_____

Title: _____

Author: _____

Date finished: _____

Note or Favorite passage: _____

_____

_____

_____

Title: _____

Author: _____

Date finished: _____

Note or Favorite passage: _____

_____

_____

_____

Title: _____

Author: _____

Date finished: _____

Note or Favorite passage: _____

_____

_____

_____

Title: _____

Author: _____

Date finished: _____

Note or Favorite passage: _____

_____

_____

_____

Title: _____

Author: _____

Date finished: _____

Note or Favorite passage: _____

_____

_____

_____

Title: _____

Author: _____

Date finished: _____

Note or Favorite passage: _____

_____

_____

_____

Title: _____

Author: _____

Date finished: _____

Note or Favorite passage: _____

_____

_____

_____

Title: _____

Author: _____

Date finished: _____

Note or Favorite passage: _____

_____

_____

_____

Title: _____

Author: _____

Date finished: _____

Note or Favorite passage: _____

_____

_____

_____

Title: _____

Author: _____

Date finished: _____

Note or Favorite passage: _____

_____

_____

_____

Title: _____

Author: _____

Date finished: _____

Note or Favorite passage: _____

_____

_____

_____

Title: _____

Author: _____

Date finished: _____

Note or Favorite passage: _____

_____

_____

_____

Title: _____

Author: _____

Date finished: _____

Note or Favorite passage: _____

_____

_____

_____

Title: _____

Author: _____

Date finished: _____

Note or Favorite passage: _____

_____

_____

_____

Title: _____

Author: _____

Date finished: _____

Note or Favorite passage: _____

_____

_____

_____

Title: _____

Author: _____

Date finished: _____

Note or Favorite passage: _____

_____

_____

_____

Title: _____

Author: _____

Date finished: _____

Note or Favorite passage: _____

_____

_____

_____

Title: _____

Author: _____

Date finished: _____

Note or Favorite passage: _____

_____

_____

_____

Title: _____

Author: _____

Date finished: _____

Note or Favorite passage: _____

_____

_____

_____

Title: _____

Author: _____

Date finished: _____

Note or Favorite passage: _____

_____

_____

_____

Title: _____

Author: _____

Date finished: _____

Note or Favorite passage: _____

_____

_____

_____

Title: _____

Author: _____

Date finished: _____

Note or Favorite passage: _____

_____

_____

_____

Title: _____

Author: _____

Date finished: _____

Note or Favorite passage: _____

_____

_____

_____

Title: _____

Author: _____

Date finished: _____

Note or Favorite passage: _____

_____

_____

_____

Title: _____

Author: _____

Date finished: _____

Note or Favorite passage: _____

_____

_____

_____

Title: _____

Author: _____

Date finished: _____

Note or Favorite passage: _____

_____

_____

_____

Title: _____

Author: _____

Date finished: _____

Note or Favorite passage: _____

_____

_____

_____

Title: _____

Author: _____

Date finished: _____

Note or Favorite passage: _____

_____

_____

_____

Title: _____

Author: _____

Date finished: _____

Note or Favorite passage: _____

_____

_____

_____

Title: _____

Author: _____

Date finished: _____

Note or Favorite passage: _____

_____

_____

_____

Title: _____

Author: _____

Date finished: _____

Note or Favorite passage: _____

_____

_____

_____

Title: _____

Author: _____

Date finished: _____

Note or Favorite passage: _____

_____

_____

_____

Title: _____

Author: _____

Date finished: _____

Note or Favorite passage: _____

_____

_____

_____

Title: _____

Author: _____

Date finished: _____

Note or Favorite passage: _____

_____

_____

_____

Title: _____

Author: _____

Date finished: _____

Note or Favorite passage: _____

_____

_____

_____

Title: _____

Author: _____

Date finished: _____

Note or Favorite passage: _____

_____

_____

_____

Title: _____

Author: _____

Date finished: _____

Note or Favorite passage: _____

_____

_____

_____

Title: _____

Author: _____

Date finished: _____

Note or Favorite passage: _____

_____

_____

_____

Title: _____

Author: _____

Date finished: _____

Note or Favorite passage: _____

_____

_____

_____

Title: _____

Author: _____

Date finished: _____

Note or Favorite passage: _____

_____

_____

_____

Title: _____

Author: _____

Date finished: _____

Note or Favorite passage: _____

_____

_____

_____

Title: _____

Author: _____

Date finished: _____

Note or Favorite passage: _____

_____

_____

_____

Title: _____

Author: _____

Date finished: _____

Note or Favorite passage: _____

_____

_____

_____

Title: _____

Author: _____

Date finished: _____

Note or Favorite passage: _____

_____

_____

_____

Title: _____

Author: _____

Date finished: _____

Note or Favorite passage: _____

_____

_____

_____

Title: _____

Author: _____

Date finished: _____

Note or Favorite passage: _____

_____

_____

_____

Title: _____

Author: _____

Date finished: _____

Note or Favorite passage: _____

_____

_____

_____

Title: _____

Author: _____

Date finished: _____

Note or Favorite passage: _____

_____

_____

_____

Title: _____

Author: _____

Date finished: _____

Note or Favorite passage: _____

_____

_____

_____

Title: _____

Author: _____

Date finished: _____

Note or Favorite passage: _____

_____

_____

_____

Title: _____

Author: _____

Date finished: _____

Note or Favorite passage: _____

_____

_____

_____

Title: _____

Author: _____

Date finished: _____

Note or Favorite passage: _____

_____

_____

_____

Title: _____

Author: _____

Date finished: _____

Note or Favorite passage: _____

_____

_____

_____

Title: _____

Author: _____

Date finished: _____

Note or Favorite passage: _____

_____

_____

_____

Title: _____

Author: _____

Date finished: _____

Note or Favorite passage: _____

_____

_____

_____

Title: _____

Author: _____

Date finished: _____

Note or Favorite passage: _____

_____

_____

_____

Title: _____

Author: _____

Date finished: _____

Note or Favorite passage: _____

_____

_____

_____

Title: _____

Author: _____

Date finished: _____

Note or Favorite passage: _____

_____

_____

_____

Title: _____

Author: _____

Date finished: _____

Note or Favorite passage: _____

_____

_____

_____

Title: _____

Author: _____

Date finished: _____

Note or Favorite passage: _____

_____

_____

_____

Title: _____

Author: _____

Date finished: _____

Note or Favorite passage: _____

_____

_____

_____

Title: _____

Author: _____

Date finished: _____

Note or Favorite passage: _____

_____

_____

_____

Title: _____

Author: _____

Date finished: _____

Note or Favorite passage: _____

_____

_____

_____

Title: _____

Author: _____

Date finished: _____

Note or Favorite passage: _____

_____

_____

_____

Title: _____

Author: _____

Date finished: _____

Note or Favorite passage: _____

_____

_____

_____

Title: _____

Author: _____

Date finished: _____

Note or Favorite passage: _____

_____

_____

_____

Title: _____

Author: _____

Date finished: _____

Note or Favorite passage: _____

_____

_____

_____

Title: _____

Author: _____

Date finished: _____

Note or Favorite passage: _____

_____

_____

_____

Title: _____

Author: _____

Date finished: _____

Note or Favorite passage: _____

_____

_____

_____

Title: _____

Author: _____

Date finished: _____

Note or Favorite passage: _____

_____

_____

_____

Title: _____

Author: _____

Date finished: _____

Note or Favorite passage: _____

_____

_____

_____

Title: _____

Author: _____

Date finished: _____

Note or Favorite passage: _____

_____

_____

_____

Title: _____

Author: _____

Date finished: _____

Note or Favorite passage: _____

_____

_____

_____

Title: _____

Author: _____

Date finished: _____

Note or Favorite passage: _____

_____

_____

_____

Title: _____

Author: _____

Date finished: _____

Note or Favorite passage: _____

_____

_____

_____

Title: _____

Author: _____

Date finished: _____

Note or Favorite passage: _____

_____

_____

_____

Title: _____

Author: _____

Date finished: _____

Note or Favorite passage: _____

_____

_____

_____

Title: _____

Author: _____

Date finished: _____

Note or Favorite passage: _____

_____

_____

_____

Title: _____

Author: _____

Date finished: _____

Note or Favorite passage: _____

_____

_____

_____

Title: _____

Author: _____

Date finished: _____

Note or Favorite passage: _____

_____

_____

_____

Title: _____

Author: _____

Date finished: _____

Note or Favorite passage: _____

_____

_____

_____

Title: _____

Author: _____

Date finished: _____

Note or Favorite passage: _____

_____

_____

_____

Title: _____

Author: _____

Date finished: _____

Note or Favorite passage: _____

_____

_____

_____

Title: _____

Author: _____

Date finished: _____

Note or Favorite passage: _____

_____

_____

_____

Title: _____

Author: _____

Date finished: _____

Note or Favorite passage: _____

_____

_____

_____

Title: _____

Author: _____

Date finished: _____

Note or Favorite passage: _____

_____

_____

_____

Title: _____

Author: _____

Date finished: _____

Note or Favorite passage: _____

_____

_____

_____

Title: _____

Author: _____

Date finished: _____

Note or Favorite passage: _____

_____

_____

_____

Title: _____

Author: _____

Date finished: _____

Note or Favorite passage: _____

_____

_____

_____

Title: _____

Author: _____

Date finished: _____

Note or Favorite passage: _____

_____

_____

_____

Title: _____

Author: _____

Date finished: _____

Note or Favorite passage: _____

_____

_____

_____

Title: _____

Author: _____

Date finished: _____

Note or Favorite passage: _____

_____

_____

_____

Title: _____

Author: _____

Date finished: _____

Note or Favorite passage: _____

_____

_____

_____

Title: _____

Author: _____

Date finished: _____

Note or Favorite passage: _____

_____

_____

_____

Title: _____

Author: _____

Date finished: _____

Note or Favorite passage: _____

_____

_____

_____

Title: _____

Author: _____

Date finished: _____

Note or Favorite passage: _____

_____

_____

_____

Title: _____

Author: _____

Date finished: _____

Note or Favorite passage: _____

_____

_____

_____

Title: _____

Author: _____

Date finished: _____

Note or Favorite passage: _____

_____

_____

_____

Title: _____

Author: _____

Date finished: _____

Note or Favorite passage: _____

_____

_____

_____

Title: _____

Author: _____

Date finished: _____

Note or Favorite passage: _____

_____

_____

_____

Title: _____

Author: _____

Date finished: _____

Note or Favorite passage: _____

_____

_____

_____

Title: _____

Author: _____

Date finished: _____

Note or Favorite passage: _____

_____

_____

_____

Title: _____

Author: _____

Date finished: _____

Note or Favorite passage: _____

_____

_____

_____

Title: _____

Author: _____

Date finished: _____

Note or Favorite passage: _____

_____

_____

_____

Title: _____

Author: _____

Date finished: _____

Note or Favorite passage: _____

_____

_____

_____

Title: _____

Author: _____

Date finished: _____

Note or Favorite passage: _____

_____

_____

_____

Title: _____

Author: _____

Date finished: _____

Note or Favorite passage: _____

_____

_____

_____

Title: _____

Author: _____

Date finished: _____

Note or Favorite passage: _____

_____

_____

_____

Title: _____

Author: _____

Date finished: _____

Note or Favorite passage: _____

_____

_____

_____

Title: _____

Author: _____

Date finished: _____

Note or Favorite passage: _____

_____

_____

_____

Title: _____

Author: _____

Date finished: _____

Note or Favorite passage: _____

_____

_____

_____

Title: _____

Author: _____

Date finished: _____

Note or Favorite passage: _____

_____

_____

_____

Title: _____

Author: _____

Date finished: _____

Note or Favorite passage: _____

_____

_____

_____

Title: _____

Author: _____

Date finished: _____

Note or Favorite passage: _____

_____

_____

_____

Title: _____

Author: _____

Date finished: _____

Note or Favorite passage: _____

_____

_____

_____

Title: _____

Author: _____

Date finished: _____

Note or Favorite passage: _____

_____

_____

_____

Title: _____

Author: _____

Date finished: _____

Note or Favorite passage: _____

_____

_____

_____

Title: _____

Author: _____

Date finished: _____

Note or Favorite passage: _____

_____

_____

_____

Title: _____

Author: _____

Date finished: _____

Note or Favorite passage: _____

_____

_____

_____

Title: _____

Author: _____

Date finished: _____

Note or Favorite passage: _____

_____

_____

_____

Title: _____

Author: _____

Date finished: _____

Note or Favorite passage: _____

_____

_____

_____

Title: _____

Author: _____

Date finished: _____

Note or Favorite passage: _____

_____

_____

_____

Title: _____

Author: _____

Date finished: _____

Note or Favorite passage: _____

_____

_____

_____

Title: _____

Author: _____

Date finished: _____

Note or Favorite passage: _____

_____

_____

_____

Title: _____

Author: _____

Date finished: _____

Note or Favorite passage: _____

_____

_____

_____

Title: _____

Author: _____

Date finished: _____

Note or Favorite passage: _____

_____

_____

_____

Title: _____

Author: _____

Date finished: _____

Note or Favorite passage: _____

_____

_____

_____

Title: _____

Author: _____

Date finished: _____

Note or Favorite passage: _____

_____

_____

_____

Title: _____

Author: _____

Date finished: _____

Note or Favorite passage: _____

_____

_____

_____

Title: _____

Author: _____

Date finished: _____

Note or Favorite passage: _____

_____

_____

_____

Title: _____

Author: _____

Date finished: _____

Note or Favorite passage: _____

_____

_____

_____

Title: _____

Author: _____

Date finished: _____

Note or Favorite passage: _____

_____

_____

_____

Title: _____

Author: _____

Date finished: _____

Note or Favorite passage: _____

_____

_____

_____

Title: _____

Author: _____

Date finished: _____

Note or Favorite passage: _____

_____

_____

_____

Title: _____

Author: _____

Date finished: _____

Note or Favorite passage: _____

_____

_____

_____

Title: _____

Author: _____

Date finished: _____

Note or Favorite passage: _____

_____

_____

_____

Title: _____

Author: _____

Date finished: _____

Note or Favorite passage: _____

_____

_____

_____

Title: _____

Author: _____

Date finished: _____

Note or Favorite passage: _____

_____

_____

_____

Title: _____

Author: _____

Date finished: _____

Note or Favorite passage: _____

_____

_____

_____

Title: _____

Author: _____

Date finished: _____

Note or Favorite passage: _____

_____

_____

_____

Title: _____

Author: _____

Date finished: _____

Note or Favorite passage: _____

_____

_____

_____

Title: _____

Author: _____

Date finished: _____

Note or Favorite passage: _____

_____

_____

_____

Title: _____

Author: _____

Date finished: _____

Note or Favorite passage: _____

_____

_____

_____

Title: _____

Author: _____

Date finished: _____

Note or Favorite passage: _____

_____

_____

_____

Title: _____

Author: _____

Date finished: _____

Note or Favorite passage: _____

_____

_____

_____

Title: _____

Author: _____

Date finished: _____

Note or Favorite passage: _____

_____

_____

_____

Title: _____

Author: _____

Date finished: _____

Note or Favorite passage: _____

_____

_____

_____

Title: _____

Author: _____

Date finished: _____

Note or Favorite passage: _____

_____

_____

_____

Title: _____

Author: _____

Date finished: _____

Note or Favorite passage: _____

_____

_____

_____

Title: _____

Author: _____

Date finished: _____

Note or Favorite passage: _____

_____

_____

_____

Title: _____

Author: _____

Date finished: _____

Note or Favorite passage: _____

_____

_____

_____

Title: _____

Author: _____

Date finished: _____

Note or Favorite passage: _____

_____

_____

_____

Title: _____

Author: _____

Date finished: _____

Note or Favorite passage: _____

_____

_____

_____

Title: _____

Author: _____

Date finished: _____

Note or Favorite passage: _____

_____

_____

_____

Title: _____

Author: _____

Date finished: _____

Note or Favorite passage: _____

_____

_____

_____

Title: _____

Author: _____

Date finished: _____

Note or Favorite passage: _____

_____

_____

_____

Title: _____

Author: _____

Date finished: _____

Note or Favorite passage: _____

_____

_____

_____

Title: _____

Author: _____

Date finished: _____

Note or Favorite passage: _____

_____

_____

_____

Title: _____

Author: _____

Date finished: _____

Note or Favorite passage: _____

_____

_____

_____

Title: _____

Author: _____

Date finished: _____

Note or Favorite passage: _____

_____

_____

_____

Title: _____

Author: _____

Date finished: _____

Note or Favorite passage: _____

_____

_____

_____

Title: _____

Author: _____

Date finished: _____

Note or Favorite passage: _____

_____

_____

_____

Title: _____

Author: _____

Date finished: _____

Note or Favorite passage: _____

_____

_____

_____

Title: _____

Author: _____

Date finished: _____

Note or Favorite passage: _____

_____

_____

_____

Title: _____

Author: _____

Date finished: _____

Note or Favorite passage: _____

_____

_____

_____

Title: _____

Author: _____

Date finished: _____

Note or Favorite passage: _____

_____

_____

_____

Title: _____

Author: _____

Date finished: _____

Note or Favorite passage: _____

_____

_____

_____

Title: _____

Author: _____

Date finished: _____

Note or Favorite passage: _____

_____

_____

_____

Title: _____

Author: _____

Date finished: _____

Note or Favorite passage: _____

_____

_____

_____

Title: _____

Author: _____

Date finished: _____

Note or Favorite passage: _____

_____

_____

_____

Title: _____

Author: _____

Date finished: _____

Note or Favorite passage: _____

_____

_____

_____

Title: _____

Author: _____

Date finished: _____

Note or Favorite passage: _____

_____

_____

_____

Title: _____

Author: _____

Date finished: _____

Note or Favorite passage: _____

_____

_____

_____

Title: _____

Author: _____

Date finished: _____

Note or Favorite passage: _____

_____

_____

_____

Title: _____

Author: _____

Date finished: _____

Note or Favorite passage: _____

_____

_____

_____

Title: _____

Author: _____

Date finished: _____

Note or Favorite passage: _____

_____

_____

_____

Title: _____

Author: _____

Date finished: _____

Note or Favorite passage: _____

_____

_____

_____

Title: _____

Author: _____

Date finished: _____

Note or Favorite passage: _____

_____

_____

_____

Title: _____

Author: _____

Date finished: _____

Note or Favorite passage: _____

_____

_____

_____

Title: _____

Author: _____

Date finished: _____

Note or Favorite passage: _____

_____

_____

_____

Title: _____

Author: _____

Date finished: _____

Note or Favorite passage: _____

_____

_____

_____

Title: _____

Author: _____

Date finished: _____

Note or Favorite passage: _____

_____

_____

_____

Title: _____

Author: _____

Date finished: _____

Note or Favorite passage: _____

_____

_____

_____

Title: _____

Author: _____

Date finished: _____

Note or Favorite passage: _____

_____

_____

_____

Title: _____

Author: _____

Date finished: _____

Note or Favorite passage: _____

_____

_____

_____

Title: _____

Author: _____

Date finished: _____

Note or Favorite passage: _____

_____

_____

_____

Title: _____

Author: _____

Date finished: _____

Note or Favorite passage: _____

_____

_____

_____

Title: _____

Author: _____

Date finished: _____

Note or Favorite passage: _____

_____

_____

_____

Title: _____

Author: _____

Date finished: _____

Note or Favorite passage: _____

_____

_____

_____

Title: _____

Author: _____

Date finished: _____

Note or Favorite passage: _____

_____

_____

_____

Title: _____

Author: _____

Date finished: _____

Note or Favorite passage: _____

_____

_____

_____

Title: _____

Author: _____

Date finished: _____

Note or Favorite passage: _____

_____

_____

_____

Title: _____

Author: _____

Date finished: _____

Note or Favorite passage: _____

_____

_____

_____

Title: _____

Author: _____

Date finished: _____

Note or Favorite passage: _____

_____

_____

_____

Title: _____

Author: _____

Date finished: _____

Note or Favorite passage: _____

_____

_____

_____

Title: _____

Author: _____

Date finished: _____

Note or Favorite passage: _____

_____

_____

_____

Title: _____

Author: _____

Date finished: _____

Note or Favorite passage: _____

_____

_____

_____

Title: _____

Author: _____

Date finished: _____

Note or Favorite passage: _____

_____

_____

_____

Title: _____

Author: _____

Date finished: _____

Note or Favorite passage: _____

_____

_____

_____

Title: _____

Author: _____

Date finished: _____

Note or Favorite passage: _____

_____

_____

_____

Title: _____

Author: _____

Date finished: _____

Note or Favorite passage: _____

_____

_____

_____

Title: _____

Author: _____

Date finished: _____

Note or Favorite passage: _____

_____

_____

_____

Title: _____

Author: _____

Date finished: _____

Note or Favorite passage: _____

_____

_____

_____

CPSIA information can be obtained at www.ICGtesting.com
Printed in the USA
LVOW08s1745100116

469984LV00002B/558/P